Put It

MW01592573

By Larry Osman

Illustrations by Alicia Puma

www.putitinyouract.com

Published 2009 by www.lulu.com

ISBN: 978-0-557-09545-2

*To my wonderful wife Robin and our great kids, Eric, Alex and Jamie, for being supportive during my "book" phase.*

# Table of Contents

# Urine for an Adventure

I was talking to my friend Dave on my cell phone, as we were both commuting home from our jobs. Dave, a short, stocky, salt and pepper haired fellow asked me, "What's new?"

I replied, "Not much," and we ended our brief conversation. Our lack of words indicated that we were deep within the downward spiral of a midlife crisis. Though our chat was short, I was certain it would forever change our lives.

We were both in need of something exciting and new that would take us back to those good old college days. During semester breaks, we would each eagerly drive for twenty minutes late at night, just to meet at the Roy Rogers halfway between our homes. We weren't there for Roy's famous roast beef or tasty fried chicken, but to drink coffee and chat with each other when our peers would be out rocking at the popular dance clubs.

We had way more important things to do as this was the place where Dave talked eagerly about cars with hair. "Wouldn't it be great" he asked, "If cars could grow hair? People would simply drive to the nearby *carwash/salon* to get hot wax and a little off the top."

Believe it or not, Dave was a pretty normal guy. However, he did once confide in me that his grandfather had painted his car with house paint. I wondered if he also wallpapered the car's vinyl roof. And Dave would also on occasion, take a Pep-O-Mint Life Saver, swallow it whole with a glass of water (aspirin style) and then exclaim, "Ah, that's refreshing." Besides that, I guess he was pretty normal. I miss those fun days.

That's when it hit me like a ton of bricks. We would collaborate on a book. We'd author a handy guide on a subject that's always fascinated me. The book would inform its readers of the various ways to change the color and other attributes of their own urine. As a gastroenterologist, Dave could help me in the chapter that discusses how various prescriptions and over the counter medications can change someone's pee from yellow, to orange, to brown. I'd dedicate two entire chapters to asparagus and beets respectively.

I quickly called Dave back and told him of my epiphany. "We're going to write a book all about the effect of food and drugs on urine," I exclaimed. He paused and asked if we would include the old "put a sleeping person's hand in warm water to make him pee" trick in the book. Although tempting, I let him know that this would not happen, as I really wanted to keep this literary work pure and concentrate only on how changes in color and odor were affected based on consumption of various organic and inorganic compounds. He was quite lukewarm about our prospects. He reminded me of the time I was going to write a book entitled, "*What to Expect When You're Expectorating*," a handy self help book. I disbanded that effort thinking that since a severe flu season was predicted, I'd be just yet another author following on the coattails of popular releases like "*The Idiot's Guide to Coughing*" and "*Sputum for Dummies.*"

He muttered, "I wouldn't quit my day job."

I said, "I'm being serious! Are you aware that after drinking a double espresso, my pee smells like coffee?"

He said, "Big shit, who cares?" Dave was rather practical and asked if I realistically thought that I would have enough material for an entire book. I begrudgingly asked if he thought I might have enough with his help for a pamphlet or even a tri-fold brochure. He responded that he didn't want to quit his successful medical practice for this. He thought at best, I would only have enough subject matter for a flyer that could be placed on car windshields in crowded parking lots. I didn't appreciate this as I thought he was belittling my idea, but even if he wasn't, how could I compete with all those Chinese restaurant menus (though there were some synergies with menu item #17 – Hunan asparagus)?

I did some quick research on my book's prospective title. To my amazement nobody in the course of human history has titled a literary work "Urine for an Adventure." That was a relief. However, while I was Googling the subject, I did come across a bizarre and disturbing therapy that involved the drinking of one's urine. They claim that the body is an amazing filter and there are quite a number of health benefits to this practice.

A woman had posted in the community section of a website how she tasted a drop at first and now she's up to a glass a day. I just can't picture myself coming home after a hard day's work and pouring myself a nice cold glass of piss, although I can't help but wonder what my pee would then look and smell like. In fact, I'm pretty sure that if I were to walk into a public bathroom and pee shortly after drinking my own pee, it would be so concentrated, that I might have to invoke a courtesy flush. That just doesn't happen very often at a urinal!

Readers might think that I'm preoccupied with the subject of "pee." I don't think so, however when we were expecting our third child, I did ask my wife, Robin, if we could install a urinal if number three was to be our third son. I discussed the sense of responsibility it would instill in our boys as they would have to walk up a flight of stairs each morning and fill the urinal with ice. She agreed with much enthusiasm. At least that's how I interpreted her lack of a response.

In any event, I needed to be realistic and face the facts. I wouldn't have enough quality material for a book, but it would make a decent intro chapter to a collection of my true (although somewhat embellished) stories and observations. My dreams have come true. You (like me) have just completed chapter one!

# No Good Deed Goes Unpunished

I figured out how to play the piano as a child while visiting my grandparents' home in Trenton, New Jersey. They had an old house; with an even older cellar (it was far too drab, and musty to call it something modern like a basement). At the base of the gray painted wooden stairs was an ancient piano. It was painted bright red and had chipped ivory keys. It was quite out of tune, but I didn't know any better.

I practiced every time I visited them, and they would love to listen to me. As a treat for them, I figured out how to play old Yiddish songs that reminded them of their days in the shtetls of Eastern Europe. I had an engaged audience who loved me and I wanted to play songs that pleased them and kept them listening. My loving grandparents would have been quite happy to listen to me even if I only banged my elbows on the keys. My own parents, however, wouldn't get a piano in our house. They didn't want any noise, so I practiced every time we visited Grandma Rose and Grandpa Sol. One day I hoped I could spread joy to others by playing my Klezmer-inspired music.

That time was to occur 35 years later in Greenwich, Connecticut. I had to attend a work meeting at the Westchester, New York regional office of my company. My boss had taken me to a very cool modern Pan Asian restaurant that served exotic food and played house music that got louder with every passing hour. I told my wife Robin all about this extraordinary place. It was nothing like any dining establishments we had in New Jersey. It was trendy, tropical, contemporary and had amazing martinis. I ate there with my boss on many subsequent business trips and returned home with tales of wonderfully delicious sizzling calamari salad and wok-seared shrimp accompanied by some spicy mango chutney. We decided to plan a trip to visit the restaurant. It was two hours away, so my in-laws offered to stay at our house and watch the kids. We drove up one Friday after work and checked in to a beautiful hotel minutes from the restaurant.

The hotel had an open atrium with 20-foot trees that made it seem like a tropical jungle. It had a nice pool, sauna and Jacuzzi. We relaxed before we ventured out to dinner. We did however notice that there were many Hasidic Jews in the hotel, accompanied by lots of kids. They were in the lobby, at the pool and walking in the tropical gardens. They had arrived en masse to attend a wedding that was to take place on Saturday night after the Sabbath had ended. Since they couldn't drive on Saturdays, they arrived Friday afternoon and would stay on the hotel premises until after the wedding. We got in our car and drove a mile down the road to dinner.

The restaurant was amazing. We had hoisin chicken lettuce wraps, goat cheese stuffed wontons, multiple martinis, wok-fired steak with Wasabi mashed potatoes and banana spring rolls with basil-infused ice cream for dessert. We were full and slightly buzzed when we arrived back at the hotel late that Friday night. There were scores of little Hasidic kids running around with white shirts, black pants and payas (side curls). As we were approaching the hotel lobby, I noticed a grand piano. It was nothing like the one my grandparents had. This one was big, shiny, new and most likely perfectly in tune. I thought I'd entertain the little kids by playing the same songs that entertained my grandparents years before.

I began playing Yiddish songs and instead of smiling and dancing, the kids stared at me as if I had two heads. Unfazed, I continued to play, thinking that they must have been taken aback by my impressive piano playing skills. All of a sudden an older man with a long white beard, black hat and cane slowly approached me.

"What song is this you play?" asked the Hasid (like he didn't know). I proudly exclaimed that I was playing "*Shein vi de L'vone*," a Yiddish folk song popular in the 1940's which translated means, "Pretty as the Moon." "How do you know such song?" asked the inquisitive man. I told him that my grandparents sang it to me and I would play it for them on their piano. He asked, "Oh – your grandparents teach you such a song?" I nodded proudly. He then exclaimed "And your grandparents also teach you to play on Shabbos?!!" He then abruptly turned around and quickly walked into a room and shut the door.

I was shocked and it took a minute to realize that I had broken the Sabbath laws by playing a musical instrument on the day of rest. Robin, who at this point was laughing uncontrollably, quickly called her mom on her cell phone, asked how the kids were behaving, let her know that dinner was great, and explained that I had just insulted an entire branch of the Lubavitcher sect.

# Family Secret

Throughout the annals of time, man has always wanted to trace his roots. I was no different, and wanted to know where my family came from. Osman was an interesting surname. The head of the Ottoman Empire was "Osman the 1st" who ruled over the Turks starting in 1299. His empire lasted six centuries and spanned over three continents. I've worked with a number of computer professionals who attended the esteemed University of Osmania in India. Perhaps the city's founders were related to me. Friends of my parents snapped a photo of a sign in France letting visitors know they were entering Osmanville. Could we be French? I've always had what seemed like a genetic liking for Jerry Lewis. Maybe I'm a distant relative of the Buffalo Bills quarterback, J.P. Losman. My relatives might have shortened it by dropping the "L" when coming to America. A number of recent terrorists have also shared the surname of Osman. Some even had the first, middle and last name of Osman. How did this infamous name relate to my particular family?

Grandpa Max wasn't a terrorist or the ruler of an empire, and the only relation to a quarterback was when he grabbed the extra 25 cents that his companion left as a tip at the local deli (he had erroneously tipped on the full amount including tax and liquor). He lived in a tiny apartment in Brooklyn and after retiring at 63, spent the last thirty years of his life sitting on lawn furniture watching TV in the small area between the kitchen and the bedroom. He was a pioneer at multitasking and was able to watch TV, smoke a pipe and yell in Yiddish at my Grandma Gussie all at the same time. Their marriage of over 60 years, coupled with their close quarters, led to some rather loud yelling that was heard five floors below on the street in front of their building. Once my family parked in front of their apartment and heard the sound of my grandfather calling my grandmother a *behema* (Yiddish for oxen). She would in turn say that many men died young of heart attacks and cancer or even automobile accidents. "Max!!! Die already!" Was this the same lineage as the warriors of the Ottoman Empire? It was time to find out.

That time came decades after Max and Gussie passed on at the ripe ages of 93 and 86 respectively. I was home with some virus that I must have caught from my kids and I didn't have the desire to do anything but Google the Osman name. I stumbled across some genealogy sites and upon paying $19.95 with PayPal, I was eagerly creating our family tree. I thought this would be a welcome gift for my children. So far they haven't appreciated my other gifts that would be passed down from generation to generation. In fact, when I die, I'm sure they will fight with each other over which one will be stuck with my Mr. Peanut collection.

I entered my name, birth date and place of birth into the online family tree program. I did this for my wife, my sister, parents and every other family member I could think of. Then I bothered my parents for details about relatives. They told stories about my dad's cousin who was called "Little Head." They thought his name was really Melvin, but nobody was sure how he was related to us. My aunt gave me a picture of my Grandpa Max with his family when he was a child in Warsaw, Poland. There were six brothers and sisters and their parents. One of the boys was holding a picture frame of their oldest brother who had already come to America.

Dad was not too happy with my obsession with genealogy. He said disapprovingly, "Why are you doing this? They're all dead and you aren't going to make any money from this. Why do you care about them?" I told him I was doing it for my kids so they would know where they came from. He wasn't impressed.

*This page intentionally left blank*

After entering the details of my family tree online, I was notified that another family had a tree similar to mine, and there might be a connection. I traded emails with a nice woman from Nebraska whose Grandfather Joseph seemed to be my grandfather's brother. She had my grandfather in her family tree and his wife Gussie. How many Max and Gussie Osmans could there be? She did not have my father or my aunt, but she did have my Uncle Willie. I was excited that this Cornhusker was a relative! I thought that Nebraska was a long way from Poland.

I emailed her the picture I had from the old country. She was quite pleased and wrote back to me confirming that the man in the picture seated next to my grandfather, was indeed her grandfather. The rest of her email was quite disturbing. I let my 11 year-old son Alex read it out loud. "Thanks for the photo. It's nice to hear from another Osman relative. My grandfather had an extra finger on each hand. Many of my cousins were born with extra digits. My daughter was born with an extra finger on each hand and an extra toe on each foot. Do any in your family have extra digits?" My son became spooked as if he had just watched his first horror movie.

I asked Alex if he thought I should host an Osman family reunion so we could meet all of our long lost relatives. We'd all have nametags, many of which would have the surname Osman upon them. He said he didn't want to give anyone there a high six. I kind of agreed with him and we joked that there would be events like typing contests and workshops on how to play the sitar.

Later that evening, I studied the photo taken way back in 1912 and zoomed in using Photoshop. I was searching for extra fingers. Lo and behold, Joseph's hands were tucked neatly behind his back hiding the family secret. I told my dad of the news and he said "Now are you happy?"

# Location, Location, Location

It wasn't until I was married that I actually enjoyed vacations. You see, growing up, our vacations were not something that would make it on to an episode of "Lifestyles of the Rich and Famous." Exotic, hypnotic and lush were not descriptions often given to the hotels that we visited in the Amish country in Pennsylvania, or the Catskills in upstate New York or even the hotels in beautiful Asbury Park, New Jersey. It's not that the places my parents took us to weren't fun; it's just that the idea of a vacation was quite stressful to my father and in turn to the entire family.

My sister and I would usually get into fights in the backseat of the car. These were usually caused when she crossed the imaginary line that separated our personal spaces. My mom would yell and threaten that my dad would pull over. He never did. When we arrived at the hotel, my father would search our room for problems. He would find a stain on the carpet, a fly in the room or the ever-present view of the generator. He'd then focus on this for the entire stay. We once spent spring break in the Catskills, not realizing that the laws of Passover were in effect. The normally great food was lacking something. That something was bread. The kid's pizza was rather soggy when it was cheese and sauce on matzo. There weren't any cookies, strudel or brownies to be had. After a few years of unsatisfying family trips, Dad was convinced that we didn't have to travel far for a vacation, for the best things were just minutes from our house. Unfortunately that's when the light bulb in his head went on. "Family," he said, "we will vacation next summer at the Edison Holiday Inn."

At first we thought he was joking, for this hotel was only about a mile and a half from our house and even shared the same zip code. He said it had a beautiful pool and a game room and there wouldn't be any fighting on the trip there since it would only take three minutes to drive there (four if the light on Route 1 was red). Since we lived in the area, we knew where all the good restaurants were and he would be able to drive home everyday to get the mail and the newspaper. Who could argue with this logic?

We checked in, went up to the room and unpacked everything into the dresser drawers as if we were going to live there for a month. We were tired and hungry after the long drive (our version of jetlag). We piled back in the car to venture out for dinner. We arrived at Mama Maria's Italian restaurant. There wasn't a close parking spot in front, so Dad dropped us off and went to park the car. The hostess seated the three of us, gave us menus, bread and filled our water glasses. A few minutes later, my dad walked in and said to Mom, "What kind of table is this? It has a view of the men's room." He summoned for the waitress and we made our way to a more pleasant table, each of us holding our own menu, buttered roll and glass of water. This ritual was repeated at many fine dining establishments throughout the tri-state area. We then decided what to order. Dad proclaimed that he was going to have the veal parmigiana. I said I would also have it. My dad quickly changed his order to the veal marsala. We were never allowed to get more than one of the same item. The logic was, if one dish was a "loser," we'd all be stuck with it.

We enjoyed our dinner and my folks asked us if we were enjoying our vacation. It was a bit odd being at the same restaurant we'd dined at many times before, only this time, we were on vacation, but I didn't dwell on that paradox. The check came, and my dad (a Certified Public Accountant) examined it closely. He always had to find the mistake that he claimed was ever present in a check. As soon as he spotted it, he'd give me the check and say, "Can you find the mistake?" I usually couldn't and he'd exclaim, "They charged us for five sodas but we only had four." or "That special was supposed to include soup." This time it was just a simple addition error of 14 cents. It was rectified and he came out victorious. We drove back to the hotel and my parents sat in the lobby and chatted, while my sister and I hung out in the game room. This vacation was actually pretty fun.

The idea of staying local made sense to us, at least until we went out to the pool the next afternoon and my mom was chatting with another lady who was there with her kids. She had just flown in from Ohio as they were looking at houses in the area since her husband was being transferred to New Jersey. She asked Mom where she was from. That's when the embarrassment kicked in. My mother sheepishly told the woman that she had lived in Edison for the past 15 years. Yes, the same town where the hotel was located. She then confessed that her husband had just driven home to get the mail. She hid the stack of "Edison Holiday Inn" post cards that she was in the midst of writing to friends and relatives. When Dad came back four minutes later (yes, the light on Route 1 was red), we got out of the pool, dried off, packed, checked out and drove home. It was good to be back home.

# Thou Shalt Not Do It Yourself

When I met my prospective father-in-law, he began to ask me questions about my car. "How often do you change the oil?"

I said, "Every 2,500 miles."

He then said, "Do you use 10-W40?" I nodded affirmatively. I guess it was the correct answer. He then asked if I change it myself and dispose of the oil properly. I didn't answer his question; I just excused myself and walked to be with my girlfriend (wife to be). I actually changed my oil every six months whether it needed it or not, and not by myself, but by bringing it to Jiffy Lube. I was not even close to being handy. I needed help just opening the hood. Even if it was open, which cap had to be removed to check the oil anyway?

My dad grew up in Brooklyn in an apartment and they always called the super if anything needed fixing. In fact, our next-door neighbor once told me that after the first snow storm hit shortly after my parents moved in, Dad was out there trying to shovel the snow with a rake. Once I got married, I was determined to try to do things by myself. I wanted not only the personal satisfaction of self-accomplishment, but it would be a lot cheaper than paying somebody to do all the work around our house.

Years later when Robin and I were living in a condo, I started small by hanging pictures, and installing child safety plug blockers and night lights after the birth of our first son. I was even able to put together desks and TV stands, although this would usually be a full day's effort and I always had many extra parts left over. I got better and better at being handy. When we were moving into a house due to our growing family, I removed one of the wire shelves I had put up in the garage of our condo. Shortly thereafter, I noticed a leak in the garage. Every time someone flushed a toilet or took a shower, water would drip out of the wall of the garage. We called a plumber and he snaked the drain all the way to the street. This didn't help. Then he ripped out a portion of the drywall in the garage and exclaimed, "Hey someone drilled a hole into the water pipe." I guess I was that someone who installed a shelf into the pipe that removed our condo's wastewater. It wasn't until I removed the shelf that the leak started. Saving the $5 shelf cost me $250 in plumber costs. This was a pattern that I would continue to repeat.

*This page intentionally left blank*

Years later, I was trying to remove a few dead tree branches from some old trees in our backyard. The dead wood was about 25 feet up from the base of the tree and I figured the best way to get these limbs down was to wrap some rope around them and just pull. How was I going to get a rope 25 feet up a tree? My son started to climb the tree and made it up around 10 feet when he gave up. I then had the smart idea to tie one end of the rope firmly around the head of a heavy hammer. Then I tried throwing the hammer up in the air hoping it would clear the dead branches. My first 10 attempts failed and my eleventh toss went straight up in the air, and the hammer tied to the rope came down quickly just missing our heads. We then put on our bicycle helmets and tried again. Eventually, the hammer got wedged 25 feet up the tree, and no matter how hard we pulled, it wouldn't come down. When we finally had to hire a guy to cut down the dead trees, he said "Check it out, there's a hammer and rope up in this tree."

I said, "Wow, that's weird."

One summer evening, I was eating outside on our deck with my family. There were many flies interrupting our peaceful dinner and freaking out Robin and the kids. Later that night I went to Home Depot and bought a fly trap, determined to rid ourselves of these pests. I came home and added some liquid bait into the plastic container with holes on the lid (for the flies to enter and perish). The next morning, I awoke at 6:00 AM and went outside to check the trap. It was amazing! The jar was full of flies. There must have been over a hundred. There wasn't enough room to fit even the skinniest of flies.

I brought the full trap inside to dump the dead flies down the toilet so I could put the trap back outside and collect more. The only problem was that upon opening the jar, I realized that the flies were not yet dead and the bait smelled like shit. (There was some truth to the expression "like flies on shit.") Flies were buzzing around the bathroom and I had to run out due to the overwhelming stench. My poor wife, who was trying to enjoy sleeping in on this particular Sunday morning (now 6:10 AM), was awakened by my screams, the horrible smell, and multitudes of flies buzzing throughout the house. She wondered who in his right mind would try to re-use a fly trap?

A few years after the fly incident, I noticed some

rustling every time I took the garbage cans to the curb. There always seemed to be some movement underneath one shrub growing alongside our driveway. One day I was able to make out what appeared to be a gopher. I was determined, like Bill Murray in Caddy Shack, to get rid of this varmint. I found the perfect product at a trip to the hardware store. It was called Gopher-Gassers. It looked like a stick of dynamite. You simply light the fuse, place it in the gopher hole, and presto, no more gophers!

My neighbor across the street was getting her mail when she noticed that I had a lighter and what looked like some fireworks. She asked me what I was doing and I told her about our problem and my ingenious solution. She asked if she could watch. I said, "Sure, come on over!" I lit the fuse and couldn't determine where the gopher hole actually was, so I just tossed the gasser where I had seen the destructive animal in the past. The gasser did what gassers do. It emitted a thick white smoke and I had trouble even seeing my neighbor who was standing on the other side of the bush. She asked if it was supposed to be so smoky. I said, "Sure, that's what gets the gophers." She then asked if I smelled something burning.

It quickly became apparent that the entire bush was on fire. It was embarrassing when another neighbor who was a member of the volunteer fire department drove over and helped extinguish the fire. After everyone left, I noticed the gopher. He had simply moved out of the way to another nearby shrub that wasn't burnt to the ground.

The image of the burning bush brought me back to biblical times. If there were an eleventh commandment for the children of Israel, it would have been "Thou shalt not do it yourself."

Recently, Robin noticed that her minivan in the driveway had a severe flat tire. I didn't want to break the eleventh commandment, so when she asked if I could help fix it, I persuaded her to call AAA, quickly parked my car in the garage, and hid in the basement until the tow truck operator arrived and finished changing the flat.

# The Fine Art of Mentoring

After graduating from college, I accepted a job working for a medium-sized telecommunications company located in northern New Jersey, just minutes from the George Washington Bridge. The work was interesting, but my boss much more interesting. Picture, if you will, a large man, extremely disheveled, with thick Coke bottle glasses and a seedy mustache. He was about 100 pounds overweight and a complete slob. He cursed like a drunken sailor and had a high-pitched voice similar to Maxwell Smart, the character Don Adams played in "Get Smart". Ryan Mavis wasn't just a disgusting and bizarre man; he was my mentor and taught me about life in the real world, or at least his version of it.

I learned much about the business world, the telecommunications industry and the new and exciting field of personal computer programming. I loved my job and excelled at my new career. Ryan would often take me to Japanese and Korean restaurants in Fort Lee and he introduced me to sushi way before it was popular with non-Asians. Actually, I would take him, since he was legally blind and could not drive. We had many memorable lunchtime excursions sampling all sorts of global culinary styles. We tried Afghan, Armenian, Thai, and really authentic Chinese. We were always the only non-Afghani, non-Korean and non (fill in the blank) at these authentic ethnic dining establishments we visited. We'd dine on uni, slurp up snails with small straws and sample cold pigeon in wine sauce. The pigeon served was cut into small pieces, and then reassembled back together with toothpicks including the feet and head (with a prominent beak attached). I feared that I'd get the leg with the note, but Ryan assured me that they didn't serve carrier pigeons. We received many stares from the other diners as Ryan had an immense presence (literally) and would usually emerge at the end of a meal covered in stains and rubbing his huge stomach in a satisfied manner.

One day he informed me that he and Devon Kenning (another husky chap who tipped the scales at just over 300 pounds) were visiting Hank's Franks for lunch. They said it was the White Castle of hot dogs. We piled into the cab of Devon's pickup truck (a tight fit) and made our way to this frankfurter Mecca. Upon arrival, both Ryan and Devon pointed to a small rusty sign on the wall and ordered the "special". The sign said "Buy nine Texas wieners and get the 10th for free." I followed their lead but ordered only six Texas wieners as I could easily inhale six White Castle sliders at a sitting. However, when they called our number, I noticed full-sized hot dogs, covered with mounds of chili, mustard and raw onions. I had my pride on the line, and struggled to finish all six. Of course the others downed their 10 wieners quickly. Unfortunately, due to the high quantity of food consumed, we couldn't all fit in the front of the pickup for the return trip to the office. I had to sit in the bed of truck (with my suit and tie on mind you) and hold on for dear life. After we got back to the office, I asked my boss if I could leave early, as I didn't feel very well.

Ryan was a bizarre character. He used to sit in his office in the morning and devour a few powdered sugar doughnuts. This was most likely his second or third breakfast of the day. He bought them wrapped in plastic and since his vision was poor, he wolfed them down, usually spitting out small pieces of plastic wrap along the way. He would always announce that he had to pee. "Got to tap the old kidneys," he would beckon to his administrative assistant. When he would get up from his chair, there would be an outline of his shape on the floor covered with powdered sugar. It was like a police homicide investigation complete with the chalk outline of the body. The only thing missing was the police crime scene tape.

He told me stories of how he wouldn't waste his money on crappy Broadway plays; he instead would bring a bottle of wine in a paper bag and attend municipal court proceedings in Chinatown. "This, Larry, was real theatre of the absurd."

He proudly told me that the owner of one of his favorite restaurants would cover him with a table cloth not unlike a barber would put a cape around you so he wouldn't spill food on his clothes (not that this would bother him).

He also told me of one of his previous job interviews. "Larry, it was a lunch interview and just as the vice president asked me a tough question about solving simultaneous equations, my glasses fell off into my split pea soup. I quickly fetched them, licked off the soup, answered the question and got the job." This was just one of many typical Ryan Mavis experiences. I, for one, would never order split pea soup at a job interview lunch just in case I got a hard question, panicked and pulled an "Exorcist".

It was time for the first performance review of my young career. My father provided me with some advice prior to my "one on one" with my boss. "Whatever they give you as a raise, simply say thank you, but quite frankly, I expected more." I was a bit tense before my formal meeting with Ryan Mavis.

He said, "Fellow, we're quite proud of your accomplishments here during the year and I was able to get the executive board's permission to give you a 20% salary increase!" I was very happy with the news, unfortunately I responded with my dad's advice.

"Thank you very much Mr. Mavis, but quite frankly, I expected more."

Upon speaking to my dad that evening and giving him the results of my performance appraisal, he said "Twenty percent! That's amazing." After I told him my response, he said "What are you crazy? Nobody gets twenty percent!" I called my boss that evening, apologized for my bizarre reaction, and thanked him for my salary increase.

It was the early '80s, and I finally decided to purchase a VCR since the price had dropped significantly from $1,300 down to only $350 in the course of a few years. I looked forward to taping my favorite television shows, especially New York Mets games if I wasn't able to watch them live. Ryan kept asking me when I would be getting my VCR and recommended features that I doubted I would ever use. I purchased my new VCR and the next day when I arrived at work, there was a brown paper shopping bag crumpled up on my chair. Inside were about five unlabeled video cassette tapes. I wasn't quite sure what they were. Just then Ryan Mavis waddled by and said, "Hey, I got you a little present for your new toy. Enjoy." I thanked him and later that night, brought the tattered bag out when my friends were over my apartment checking out my new VCR. Not that we were overly surprised to find that each tape was filled with adult movies, we were however surprised as to the degree of explicitness and the variety of the films. The movies contained cameo roles provided by midgets, amputees and animals.

A few months later Ryan asked me if I would take him to the local post office to purchase a post office box on his behalf. It was a requirement that one must submit a driver's license with the application. Since Ryan was legally blind and could not drive, he was proposing that I open up the mailbox in my name and he would just pay me. After thinking back to those movies, I had visions of what items would arrive at the post office box in plain brown paper wrappers clearly addressed to my name. It was time to find another job.

# The Obligatory Bathroom Humor Chapter

I hate to resort to bathroom humor so early in this book, but it will pair well with the Ryan Mavis stories in the last chapter (as well as Chilean sea bass and a nice oaky, buttery California Chardonnay). You must be thinking to yourself that I resorted to it in chapter one, however I mean the real deal here; number two.

I was about 18 years old and had come home from college for spring break. My friends weren't the type to travel to Fort Lauderdale or Daytona Beach, but they also weren't interested in partying it up at the Edison Holiday Inn. I spent my days working at Burger King and my nights hanging out with my friends at clubs, arcades and eventually White Castle for a night cap.

Severe stomach pains woke me up one morning and to my dismay, both of the bathrooms were occupied. The pains were bad; I had to use the half bathroom located in my dad's office. His office was a spacious room with way too many chairs, couches and lights. There was a desk with an old typewriter where he sat when he worked. Every chair was covered with tax forms and related publications. The

*This page intentionally left blank*

bathroom was a coffin-like space behind a door at the far end of his office. It had a toilet and a roll of toilet paper and nothing else. It was the first room to flood after heavy rains and had a musty damp feel to it. It was decorated in what seemed to be a Guantanamo Bay prison motif (early Gitmo). I didn't have time to turn on any lights, as I made my way through the obstacle course of chairs to the bathroom door. I sat down and had a Maalox moment. This was payback for the beer followed by seven cheeseburgers.

While I was conducting my business, I heard the doorbell ring along with some voices. The voices were getting louder and louder. My father had entered the office with a client. This was a fairly regular occasion during tax season. Spring break was not a partying opportunity for an accountant. I heard Dad turn on all the lights and they began to review J. Robert Fox's tax return. Fox was a successful businessman and there was much to review, discuss, and the interactions became intense.

I was stuck in my seat not knowing what to do. This was going to be a lengthy meeting and my feet were beginning to fall asleep from my already long stay in the bathroom. It was going to be somewhat awkward to open the door and conduct the walk of shame in my own father's office. I reluctantly decided to go for it. I flushed, opened the door, and said whatever was the 1979 equivalent of "What's up?" They seemed surprised. Dad introduced me to his client and I sheepishly left the room. Moments later, my handiwork permeated the office where the two men were working. It overpowered them and they actually had to step outside to the street. Later that day, Dad yelled at me and said I almost lost him a lucrative account. After that day, Mom made sure the bathroom had an ample supply of air freshener.

Shortly after the office-clearing event, I was out at a dance club with a friend of mine. My friends and I would frequent the dance clubs hoping to meet girls. For my crowd this was like finding a needle in a hay stack. This particular night, we stumbled upon a fairly run down club with a nice crowd and some good music. After being wallflowers for a few bottles of beer and countless songs, I got up the nerve to ask a cute girl to dance. Surprisingly, she agreed and we made our way to the dance floor. Things were going well!

That was at least until my friend Mitch made

his way through the crowded dance floor within an earshot of me. "Larrabee?" he said in a combination of a whisper and a scream. "I need to speak to you!"

I said "What is it?" as I glared at him, angered that he was interrupting my dance. He got close enough to whisper in my ear.

"My stomach really hurts and the bathroom here is disgusting."

I quickly replied, "Deal with it Mitch. If you're in pain, just go." He said he could not as there was no door on the single stall and about 10 guys were peeing.

"Larrabee, you need to drive me to a bathroom."

I handed him my keys and said, "Just come back when you're done." My dance partner looked a bit impatient as my friend and I chatted like a pair of fifth grade girls.

He said "No way, I can't even walk let alone drive." I whispered to the girl that there was an emergency and that I'd be right back. She went back to her friends and I headed to the parking lot with Mitch limping behind me.

It was almost midnight and just about everything was closed for the night. After driving for 10 minutes, we passed a Burger King. I pulled up and Mitch went inside. I was wondering if the girl at the club would still be there when I got back or if she would even talk to me. I didn't have much time to think as Mitch came running out of the restaurant with a more worried look on his face than before. It actually was two thirds of a run and one third of a limp. His belt was still undone and his zipper was down. "Larrabee," he screamed. "Drive away! Drive away!" He said the seat was filthy and he didn't sit but squatted and began his business. Always the gentleman, Mitch invoked a courtesy flush. When he did the toilet overflowed and started to pour out all over the bathroom floor. Now I understood his concern and I peeled out of the parking lot, just as the night manager was noticing the water coming from under the men's room door.

I was laughing and asked Mitch how to get back to the club. He put a stop to my laughter by announcing that he had only started to go, and now it was much worse. At this point, I think he might have been crying, so I didn't want to argue with him. I pulled right into the local hospital's emergency entrance. While Mitch hurried into the entrance dodging between two ambulances, I parked the car and made my way to the waiting room. I was embarrassed to be there and began pacing the floor. A nurse came out and asked which patient I was waiting for. Would I tell her that I was waiting for my friend to complete his dump?  As I began to stutter, Mitch emerged, rather sweaty, but obviously relieved.  We didn't go back to the club; instead we just drove back to my apartment without speaking to each other.

I was pissed at Mitch for ruining my chances of scoring, though it was 1982, and he couldn't have known any better.  If this had happened today, he would surely have had the horse sense to check the dance club's website, in particular the FAQs about bathroom cleanliness and whether or not the stall had a working door.  He then could have, as an informed consumer, either stayed home or worn an adult diaper.

The last element of my doodie trilogy involved my former neighbor Chuck.  He was driving somewhere in central New Jersey when he too was overcome with the urgent need to defecate.  Unfortunately, there were no bathrooms in sight and he was with his wife and two young boys. Alas, he noticed an Exxon station on his left.  Without thinking or signaling, he made an illegal left turn and was promptly rear-ended by a blue

minivan occupied by a mom and her young children. He opened his door and ran away from the smoking vehicles and made a beeline to the gas station's restroom. The occupants of the minivan were in shock and thought Chuck was running to dispose of some illicit drugs or hide in from the police.

Of course there was someone in the single restroom, so Chuck kept running behind the gas station, dropped his drawers and relieved himself behind a tree. Upon completion, he ran back to see if everyone was okay. He apologized profusely as his wife and the other driver exchanged insurance information. He pleaded with her not to call the police mostly because of his embarrassment about causing the accident.

My brother-in-law at one time was in sales and had to make frequent long car rides to unfamiliar areas in his expansive territory. He had the brilliant idea of publishing a bathroom guide book for those travelling in need of a bathroom. It would be similar to the Zagat guide for restaurants as it would include ratings, reviews and distinct categories. This would enable people to find the nearest clean bathroom. Just ponder this thought; If he had written this handy pocket guide to restrooms, and Chuck had read it, his accident could have been prevented.

# Time Warp

I've noticed that people seem to keep up with the latest styles until they reach a certain age and then their fashion remains constant for the rest of their lives. My dad talks about zoot suits and parachute pants, but seems to have stopped his fashion clock in 1975. He still wears red sports jackets wherever he goes with dress pants and fancy shoes. He looks like he should be whipping out a small flashlight to assist people to their seats. He isn't a movie usher, but plays the part whenever it's time for him to go out anywhere. My mom isn't immune to this time warp either. I've never seen her wear jeans or a tee shirt. Like Dad, she also seems helplessly stuck in the '70s. My grandfathers (may they rest in peace), were stuck in 1943. They would both come to our house for a casual summer cookout. Even though it was a humid August day, they would wear three piece suits, ties, and fancy pocket watches on chains.

I never thought that this would happen to me until I was at a summer barbeque and noticed that I was the sole guest wearing shorts, white socks and sneakers. Not the cool short white sports socks, but the quasi-orthopedic white socks that go way up to the top of my calves, an inch from my knees. My shorts didn't go down to my knees, but stopped about a foot above like the NBA uniforms of the early '80s. I realized that I am stuck somewhere around 1983. That's the year of my dress; jeans and tee shirts, and my music; new wave and punk. I've since switched to the "cooler" low cut socks, although they make me feel like my regular socks have lost their elastic and dropped to my ankles. I can't get all the way to bright either and wear sandals without any socks, as it creeps me out to have my bare toenails shown in public (especially the one pinky toe nail that must have stopped receiving oxygen back in 1983 after being stepped on during a Ramones concert).

Our vocabulary can't escape the big freeze either. Those born before 1935 don't talk about wearing "jeans." They refer to them as dungarees. Suitcases are valises. Pants are trousers. Bathing suits are swimming trunks. Eyeglasses are spectacles. A party is a shindig. Working out is performing calisthenics. They don't ask for de-caf; they ask for a cup of Sanka or Postum. They also eat old style food. Folks over 60 still regularly dine on liver and onions, canned vegetables and franks and beans. They don't know from tofu, white pizza or breakfast bars. Even the same food has a retro name. They eat filberts instead of hazelnuts and their hands are still slightly reddish from years of eating pistachios. The older folks don't even take Ibuprofen. It's plain old aspirin or if really needed;

Bufferin or Alka-Seltzer.

I've also noticed that older folks attract old things. I've collected pennies since I was a kid and whenever I see my parents, they give me a Dixie cup full of pennies that they've saved for me. The pennies they give me always contain a few wheat cents (pennies minted before 1959). Nowadays, it's quite rare to get them in your change, but they must conduct business with fellow old-timers. This must be the geriatric numismatic law of attraction.

My friends and I once attended a Jewish singles weekend in the Catskills. At first we were a bit embarrassed to be there, but we figured it might be fun. When we arrived it was clear that things were different than they were back at home. My friends and I all had hair and weren't 30 pounds overweight. This never seemed to help us attract women, but at this place and time, we were studs. We sat down for a fun breakfast together but some fairly homely girls sat with us. We should have been nice to them since outside of this weekend, we knew how tough it was to be ignored by the good-looking crowd. Unfortunately, we weren't that nice.

It was time to turn our clocks back to an earlier year. We chose 1968. We decided to take on the personalities of old Jewish men, hoping that this would persuade them to exit our breakfast table and leave us alone. Jeff became Morris. Mitch was Sol. Danny was Seymour and I was Pincus. It was time to order breakfast and we ordered food like a bunch of 80 year olds. We ordered soft-boiled eggs, kippers and onions, salami and eggs and lots of pumpernickel bread. The women were getting somewhat suspicious, when we all ordered 12 ounce glasses of prune juice and gulped them down as if they were shots of tequila screaming *l'chaim* in unison. We then utilized some old time vocabulary and talked about the calisthenics we were going to perform after we waited the appropriate twenty minutes after eating. The girls got up and left us. Mission accomplished!

Later that morning we went to play some volleyball. Just when I was about to serve, I felt this urgent rumbling in my stomach. I ran back to our room as the prune juice had kicked in. I awoke on the bed after taking a recovery nap and came to the realization that this was the punishment for dissing the girls.

# Glutton Free Diet

I was quite a small skinny child. I was always among the shortest and lightest kids in my classes throughout grade school and even during high school. My grandmother always urged my mom to get my blood tested and to give me iron supplements to help spurt my growth. It was embarrassing to always be picked last for gym class, too. The two star athletes were always the captains and they would routinely choose up the best players for a given sport. It always ended up that one would choose the second to last kid remaining. He was the one with crutches or a cast and then that captain would exclaim that special phrase, "Ahhh, you're stuck with Osman."

By the time I started my first job out of college I had grown to a lofty 5' 7" and tipped the scales at 145 pounds. Amongst my family, I had become a giant, a Sampson, a freak of nature. I was like Goliath compared to their smaller statures. I eventually ended up working for a cookie company and by the time I hit 30, I started my first diet. I've been dieting on and off ever since for almost twenty years now. I've tried low carb, low fat and everything in between.

I was always looking for the secret to maintaining

a desired weight, without curbing my love for eating large quantities of good food. My mother is on a gluten free diet for health reasons (celiac disease). What I needed was to adopt a glutton free diet. On this diet, all-you-can-eat buffets and smorgasbords would be strictly prohibited. When I exercised vigorously, I ate even more. I once pondered if I could eat everything I wanted, only instead of swallowing the food; I would just simply spit it out like a seasoned tobacco chewer. Upon thinking about this option, cocktail parties would become awkward, as would formal dinners. My kids, sitting at the family dinner table, might be inclined to emulate their dad and spit out their chicken nuggets and macaroni and cheese. My wife said that if I wanted to lose ten ugly pounds, I should just cut off my head, but I needed it for my job and it also might be quite painful. I had to try a more conventional and successful weight loss technique.

I wasn't alone in my desire to shed a few pounds. My good old buddy Dave (the protagonist from chapter one) also wanted to slim down once and for all. It wasn't fair. Tall guys can always shop at the Big & Tall stores that can be found all over. However, there aren't any Short & Fat stores that cater to guys looking

*This page intentionally left blank*

for a 44 waist and 28 length pair of slacks. We decided that we would initiate a diet bet. Not just a quick diet bet, but one that we would maintain our entire lives. We would agree on individual monthly weights that we must achieve or there would be a steep financial penalty (fifty bucks) to be paid to the winner. We solved the "What if neither of us get to our desired weight?" issue by stipulating that we would both have to pay our buddy Mitch. Although Mitch is our friend, neither of us wanted him to get our hard-earned money, so we now had the incentive we needed. We would email each other our daily weights so we could track our progress. We created an extensive Excel macro to graph our key metrics. The first of every month was to be our day of reckoning.

The diet bet worked quite well as the combination of competition, potential embarrassment and losing some moolah was a good one. We both dropped about 15 pounds and have kept it off for over two years. There was, however, more than one occasion when heroics were needed to get down to my monthly weight. One day I hadn't attained my goal weight in the morning and I needed to fast until I dropped the necessary half pound. My wife wasn't happy as we were supposed spend the day at the beach to celebrate our wedding anniversary, but I thought I'd be too weak lying in the sun without eating or drinking. I did make my weight by the afternoon and we were able to celebrate with a nice romantic dinner.

One particular August 1st fell smack in the midst of a major heat wave in the Northeast. Unfortunately, I was shy by a significant two pounds. Obviously, I refrained from all food and beverages. The forecast called for record temperatures, above 100 degrees coupled with high humidity. It was a work day and I had a full schedule of conference calls. Luckily, I worked for a progressive company and had the option to work from home. I decided to first ride my bicycle for an hour before my first conference call. Afterwards, I was quite tired and sweaty, but only lost a measly half pound.

We have a sun room in our house which has no heat or air conditioning vents. I quickly shut all the windows and cranked on the small gas heater used until this day, to heat the room in the winter. The thermostat achieved 104 degrees and I began my schedule of phone calls. I was wearing a bathing suit and kept a supply of towels handy so I wouldn't sweat on my computer. After every half hour call, I would check my weight and cool off for a bit. Even though the mayor of New York City declared a heat emergency, and urged people without air conditioning to visit a shelter, I continued my battle in my makeshift sauna. I probably sounded weak on my phone calls, but I strove onward. During lunchtime, I took another bike ride and by 1:30, I had achieved my weight and was able to move inside to the air conditioned house, drink water and most importantly not have to pay Dave.

Dave has great self control and discipline. Only once did he come close to losing and was tempted to self administer the pre-colonoscopy cleanse. Instead, he opted to run on his treadmill with his winter coat and hat on. Of course, it was the middle of summer. His wife thought he was nuts. My wife now plans our social calendar with our diet bet top of mind. No all you can eat buffets are allowed in the last week of a month. Vacations are usually planned for the second week of a month, ensuring sufficient time to lose when returning home. We both know that a well balanced diet coupled with an exercise regimen would allow us to maintain our weight, but that just isn't as exciting as our bet.

# Go With the Flow

A neighbor down the street in our condo complex mentioned to me once that he never visits a barber or hair salon for a haircut opting instead to cut it himself. His wife made a bit of a face, but I admired him for his ability to "do it yourself."

One Saturday morning, I was sitting in the kitchen eating breakfast with my wife. We were going to attend a wedding on Sunday and Robin mentioned that my hair was a bit unruly. After breakfast, I drove to town to get my hair cut. I went to two barbers and a hair salon and in each place I was met with at best, a five person wait. I did not want to spend my entire Saturday morning waiting for someone to cut my hair so I returned home, grabbed a pair of kitchen shears and locked myself in our bathroom.

It was a bit tough to see the back of my head, as I snipped and combed my hair. Even while holding a mirror in one hand and looking at my reflection in the wall mirror, it was a bit awkward to cut the back. I opened the door and asked Robin if she'd straighten up the back of my hair and handed her the scissors. She had a weird look on her face and said, "You can't go to the wedding looking like this!"

I walked down the street to my neighbor Rob's condo. I explained my dilemma and asked him if he'd be able to use his haircutting system to help me fix my handiwork. He agreed that I needed help and sat me down in his kitchen to wait. He then wheeled in a vacuum, opened up a box and unrolled a hose-like contraption. He then put some plastic spacers on it and plugged it into an electric outlet. He turned it on along with the vacuum cleaner and began to move the contraption around my head. He stopped to put some tapered attachment on the cutter and within ten minutes completed his mission.

I went to the wedding the next morning and Robin and I sat alongside my parents who were also invited. My dad whispered to me, "Who cut your hair? Was it Enzo from Steinfeld?" (Dad often pronounced words somewhat differently than they were supposed to be said.) I knew he was just jealous and the next day, I ordered myself a Flowbee. I guess I should have known something was strange when I called the company, and they asked if I wanted the pet grooming system or the home haircutting system.

Within a week, my haircutting system arrived. I quickly mastered the use of the plastic spacers and for years, I regularly cut my own hair and laughed at people who paid good money to wait for a person to cut their hair. I realize now, they might have been laughing at me after seeing the back of my head.

When our two boys were young and before our daughter was born, I told my wife that I could cut their hair and we could save about $30 a month. Robin pleaded with me not to touch the boys' hair. My older son agreed with his mother and quickly said "No way," but my younger son who was three at the time, didn't fully understand what was being discussed. I brought Alex into the bathroom with me one morning, sat him down on the toilet seat lid, brought in the vacuum cleaner and the Flowbee, and told him we were going to have some fun.

As soon as I turned on all the equipment, he began to cry and flail his arms wildly. I held him down with one hand and began to Flowbee his tiny head with the other. It was like I was shearing a small sheep. Finally, I heard his cries over the sounds of the vacuum, Flowbee and bathroom fan. He got loose and ran out the bathroom door. I had only been able to cut half his head and the rightmost third of his head had a buzz cut, while the remaining portion had wavy blond locks about six inches long. He looked like a small Hare Krishna boy who was about to sell flowers at an airport.

Alex ran into his mom's arms and she consoled him. He asked her if Dad could put his hair back, but she explained that it wasn't possible. She quickly left the house to take him to a hair salon. She didn't seem her normal cheerful self. When she returned, Alex had a full buzz cut. She gave him a bath since his head itched and coddled him with a soft white hooded towel. He looked like a miniature skinhead. I asked if she was getting him ready for a local Klan meeting, but she didn't seem amused. A few days later as he was waiting for his annual checkup at the pediatrician's office, another mother whispered to Robin and asked if he was going to be alright. Since he was quite thin to begin with and had virtually no hair, she had thought he was seriously ill. Luckily, he was fine and his hair finally grew back.

# Laughter is the Best Medicine – NOT!

Nothing breaks the ice at a funeral more than uncontrollable laughter. It always seems to happen at inopportune times. It is also highly contagious.

I remember attending Sabbath services one Friday night with my family. All of a sudden I heard what sounded like my father swallowing, sneezing and coughing all at the same time. Our eyes met and he slapped his leg very hard and loud and was holding his breath. He wasn't deep in prayer, but laughter. The rabbi was in the midst of the Kaddish (the prayer for the dead), one of the most solemn moments of the service. A lady behind my dad rubbed his shoulder thinking he was grieving a recently departed loved one. My mother glared at him with a look of displeasure, her eyes transmitting acute disappointment at his actions. He in turn slammed his hand on his leg again and uttered some unrecognizable high pitched grunts. Dad wasn't proud of his behavior, but he couldn't control it.

It was many years later in a different synagogue that I was attending a friend's son's Bar Mitzvah with Robin. In the back of the sanctuary at many Bar and Bat Mitzvahs was a row or two filled with 13 year olds. Many times, they behave respectfully and quietly. Not this time. An elderly relative of the Bar Mitzvah boy had fallen asleep in the row in front of some of his friends. The kids were laughing and pointing to the soundly sleeping woman. One of the boys then took the service insert, folded it into a paper airplane and proceeded to poke the lady's blue hair with it. I nudged my wife and directed her to this immature and rude behavior. Since her best friend's son was in the middle of his chanting, I thought she would put an end to this thoughtless prank (not that I would). Instead, she began to laugh uncontrollably and was promptly escorted into the lobby by an usher.

I recently served on my county's Grand Jury. My fellow jurors and I would have to report to the courthouse every Thursday for sixteen consecutive weeks. I found the experience quite interesting and there wasn't much to trigger uncontrollable laughter until one day. There were many driving under the influence, shoplifting and forgery cases. Most of the cases were drug related.

One particular case warranted the need of the county's expert witness on drugs. A gentleman who was quite short (definitely five feet tall at

*This page intentionally left blank*

most) walked into the room. He was totally bald, somewhat muscular and wearing a fancy suit. The woman next to me positioned her pinky on the side of her lips and whispered, "Look, It's freakin' Mini-Me." I lost it. Luckily I was seated in the back of the jury room, but I had let out some snorts. I quickly disguised these grunts by coughing, but I think the prosecutor noticed my red face and nervous twitching. Just when I seemed to control it, Mini-Me hopped up and sat on the edge of a table in the room. The woman looked at me again and gave me the Mini-Me pinky sign. I somehow regained my composure and was able to participate in the vote that would indict a man of possession of a Schedule II narcotic.

To help maintain my composure when I'm ready to burst out laughing at inappropriate times, I think of situations that are not funny (besides the funeral I'm attending at the moment). I recall one night that I attended a business meeting in New York City. There was a reception afterwards and I had a few beers. It was a hot summer night and while I was waiting for my car at a parking lot, I bought a large bottle of water for the ride home. I got my car and proceeded into the Lincoln Tunnel for my trip back home to New Jersey. About half way through the tunnel, traffic was at a crawl and the usual five minutes to get through became 45 minutes. I had finished the bottle of water 20 minutes before and then had quite an urge to visit a restroom.

When my car finally emerged from the tunnel, I was extremely disappointed to see tons of traffic on the Jersey side too. By now, my bladder was about to burst and although the nearest rest area on the New Jersey Turnpike was about two miles away, it would take an hour in this gridlock. I was desperate and thought about abandoning my car and peeing on the side of the road. I decided against this as there would be about 100 witnesses and since my car was on an overpass, I could be peeing on cars below. I realized that I must relieve myself into the empty water bottle or else I'd explode. Luckily it was dark out and the cars around me couldn't see me unzipping and positioning myself appropriately.

I began to relieve myself and things were looking better, at least until I realized that I was clearly going to overflow the bottle and would need to stop midstream. This wasn't an easy feat as I had to concentrate quite hard on positioning the bottle, making sure my fellow drivers weren't suspecting anything strange, and most of all halting the flow. Just as I stopped, my foot slipped from the brake and I hit the car in front of me.

My luck, the car was a classic Mustang driven by a tall muscular tattooed guy who was already out of the car looking angrily at his bumper. He was pissed (no pun intended), and I quickly put the bottle in the cup holder, and began to zip up. I finished in the nick of time, as he was right outside my driver's window. I rolled down my window, apologized and took full responsibility for the incident. I asked if there was any damage and he shook his head no. He glanced in my vehicle and seemed to notice what looked like Mountain Dew in a Poland Springs bottle, but then just said, "Watch it pal," and got back in his car.

Now when I begin to get the giggles at a serious event, I think back to the guy approaching my window, and my smiles disappear.

# Hock A Mya Ding Ding

My friend Mitch would occasionally mutter a phrase when he had a few too many beers. As soon as he was working on beer number two, he'd look around the room to ensure that the coast was clear and then whisper "*Hock-A-Mya Ding-Ding.*" When we asked him what it meant, he would look at us very seriously and say quietly and deliberately that it was the worst Chinese curse imaginable. It meant that you should have sexual intercourse with your departed great great grandmother. Ouch! That's quite a harsh curse indeed. He warned us never to use the phrase around the company of an Asian person, as we would surely get ourselves killed. We would mock Mitch and say, "an Asian?" Why would a Korean or Japanese person understand what the Chinese phrase "*Hock-A-Mya Ding-Ding*" means? He once again warned us of the severity of this curse and said we shouldn't take any chances. We humored him and half-heartedly agreed, but often wondered why Mitch was the keeper of this ancient Chinese secret.

During my friend Dave's junior year in college, he interned in a laboratory that made shampoo and cosmetics. One of the products he worked on was the first combination shampoo and conditioner around. Dave brought a gallon jug of it to our campus apartment. The stuff was great! Dave was majoring in chemistry and this internship was right up his alley. He balanced chemical equations with ease and studied every intricacy of the periodic table of elements. He said, "Hey Larry – Do the numbers 103 and 76 mean anything to you?"

I said, "Should they?" He said "They are atomic numbers of the elements that equate to your name, Lawrence Osman." I looked at the chart and lo and behold, Lawrencium and Osmium were in positions 103 and 76 respectively. Maybe my folks used a chemistry book instead of a baby name book to choose my name. Dave often day-dreamed about the day he would discover a new element. He envisioned a periodic table with his newly discovered element being showcased right below the noble gases (he was into bathroom humor too). It would be called Bill, and its symbol would be [Wm]. Ah, but I digress (like this book isn't one big-arsed digression).

One of Dave's fellow lab workers was a Chinese guy named Yapo Fong. A few weeks later, Dave approached him and asked if he would assist him. Yapo said in broken English, "Ah, sure. What you want?"

Dave was a bit scared and cautioned his friend. "What I'm about to say is quite bad. I don't want to offend you."

"Ah, you no bother me. Just say it."

Dave gulped and then whispered, "*Hock-A-Mya Ding-Ding.*"

Yapo abruptly uttered "Huh?"

It scared Dave even more, but once again he said "*Hock-A-Mya Ding-Ding.*"

This time Yapo, said "Whaaaaaat? Huka Myra ding ding? That don't mean nothing!!!" He then went on to assure Dave that this was nothing but gibberish and didn't even sound like any real Chinese words in any of the dialects he knew. Dave let us in on his interaction with Yapo and equipped with this new knowledge, we thought we'd have some fun with Mitch.

Our gang of friends spent many late nights going to nightclubs that played only 80's music. This wasn't that odd, as it was the '80s. It's actually odd that there are places today that play 80's music. We'd get there about 9:30, settle down and get some drink-e-poos. The place would begin to get crowded at 10:00 and at 10:10, we'd be ready to leave. Unfortunately there was always one of us who was working up the nerve to pursue a cute girl.

Inevitably, the girl would have shown no reciprocal interest. This futile effort would take about two hours with the rest of us waiting impatiently.

After leaving the clubs sometime past midnight we would have a strong urge to stuff our faces. All that rejection made us hungry. If we were tired, we'd stay local and hit a diner or White Castle. Occasionally, we'd take the trek to Chinatown in New York City. Restaurants there were open until 3:00 AM! We'd choose the ones with roast ducks hanging from the windows. In the most authentic dining establishments, we were the only non-Chinese patrons.

When we were out and about, Mitch would always be on the hunt for celebrities. Once at a bar, he was convinced that Neil Armstrong was right across from us. I asked him how he recognized him without his space suit on. Mitch claimed he heard him order a vodka & Tang and that's what all the astronauts drink.

Mitch's faux-celebs were usually spot on. He would find regular folks who looked like Humphrey Bogart, Phil Silvers, Elvis Costello and Phyllis Diller. The problem sometimes was we didn't know who the actual celebrity was. He'd make sure the coast was clear and then whisper, "Don't look now, but there's Herschel Bernardi at the booth in the corner eating Moo Shu Pork." None of us even knew who

Herschel Bernardi was, so we couldn't comment on how close of a match it was. Our waiter this particular evening looked like a Chinese version of Mick Jagger. Since we were now equipped with the truth about *Hock-A-Mya Ding-Ding*, we thought we'd punk Mitch.

We ordered beef chow fun, roast duck, and roast pork fried rice and a round of Cokes. All the food was served within a few minutes, but the sodas never arrived. Every time we tried to get Mick's attention, he ignored us. That's when I whispered to Mitch, that I was going to yell "*Hock-A-Mya Ding-Ding.*" That would surely get us our sodas. Mitch abruptly lost his smile, stopped scoping out other celebrities, sternly reprimanded us and urged us not to fool around with this ancient curse especially in Chinatown. I said "That's nice Mitch, but we're thirsty." I then said loudly to the waiter, "*Hock-A-Mya Ding-Ding!* We never got our Cokes!" Mitch sprang up to his feet and apologized emphatically to the confused waiter, the other Chinese patrons and anyone else who was around. He was sure we were all going to be jumped and hit upside our heads with nunchucks. We fell off of our chairs laughing and Mr. Jagger promptly returned to our table with four Cokes. Mitch was relieved, but also shocked. Dave then revealed to him that it "*don't mean nothing.*"

# The Dreaded Holiday Dilemma

One year during high school, I was invited to a close friend's house to celebrate Christmas Eve. I was a bit apprehensive, as I had never attended a Christian religious dinner. I wasn't sure what to expect. It ends up; Frank's family was a lot like mine. The main theme of the celebration was the family, friends and most of all, the food. Frank's Mom made macaroni with crab, lobster tails, flounder, and the best eggplant parmesan this side of the Atlantic. She even made kielbasa for her nephew of Polish descent. Frank had an uncle there that Mitch would have said looked like a poor man's Henry Kissinger.

In the neighborhood where I grew up in, just about everyone was either Jewish or Italian. Everyone's grandparents were from the old country and had thick accents. It seemed that Jews and Italians were quite similar, although I'd have to say Italians have better food. Frank would always pronounce Italian food like he was right off the boat. Calamari was calamad. Ricotta was ri-gut. Cappicola was gabba-gool. And most importantly, tomato sauce came from a jar. Gravy was the homemade red covering adorning Frank's family's macaroni. I felt compelled to correct Frank when we dined together at a kosher deli. I told him that it's not pronounced pastrami, but pastram!

Frank's family made me feel very comfortable and I didn't think twice about being the token Jewish guy at the holiday table. One subsequent Christmas Eve, I attended midnight mass with my Filipino girlfriend Miki, and an entourage consisting of her brothers and sisters, their boyfriends and girlfriends, and her parents. This was the first time I ever visited a church, but after dining with Frank's family, I thought I'd be fine.

Miki's father gave all ten of us crisp dollar bills. Then everyone went up for Holy Communion. I felt lonely standing there all by myself. When they returned, someone was passing around a large plate. Members of the congregation were putting money in it and all of Miki's brothers and sisters put their crisp dollar bills onto the plate. They all looked at me, while I sheepishly reached into my back pocket, pulled out my wallet and took out the dollar bill I received earlier and placed it on the collection plate. I had thought the dollar bill given to each child was the Christmas version of Hanukkah gelt. My girlfriend was slightly embarrassed and her father must have been questioning why she had to bring her Jewish boyfriend to the service.

During one holiday season, I found myself at a local hardware superstore with my son. Eric was three at the time and he was sitting in the shopping cart as I walked up and down the aisles looking for a replacement toilet seat. Eric was starting to use the "potty" and we wanted to get a child's seat, so he wouldn't fall in. As soon as he laid his eyes on the Garfield toilet seat, he was mesmerized. He asked if we could get it. It was about ten dollars more expensive than a regular child's seat. I tried to talk him out of it, but to no avail. I then said that since we hadn't bought him all of his eight Hanukkah gifts yet, if he really wanted the special Garfield seat, it would be his eighth gift. He eagerly agreed.

As we were proceeding to the checkout area, a nice little old lady approached us. She smiled at Eric and asked him if he was a good boy and what he wanted Santa to bring him for Christmas. As I began to wonder how to respond, he simply stated, "We celebrate Hanukkah."

The lady quickly smiled at Eric and said, "Well I'm sure you are a good boy and your parents will get you some great gifts for Hanukkah."

He then proudly showed the lady the toilet seat and said, "This is my favorite Hanukkah present from my parents!" The lady walked away. She probably then recognized me as the guy who tried to pocket the dollar bill at midnight mass years ago.

# Kids Say the Darnedest Things

When we were expecting our first child, my wife and I discussed baby names. We chose not to determine the sex of our unborn child. This would mean that we would need to come up with names for both a boy and a girl. According to Jewish tradition, a child is named after a recently departed relative (and I don't mean one that just took a bus to Atlantic City last week with a roll of quarters) so as to honor him or her. That was all well and good, but like a bad game of Scrabble, we just didn't have good letters to work with. If we named our child after my Great Uncle Yussel (may he rest in peace), our son could have been named Yanni or our daughter could have been named Yoko. Our ultrasound already confirmed that our fetus would be picked last in gym class, so having poor little Yanni or Yoko waiting until all the other children were picked for crab soccer teams would be cruel and unusual punishment.

We contemplated taking matters into our own hands. We would simply choose a relative whose name began with the first letter of the name we liked and kill him. As intriguing as this plan was, it was dismissed, as if we got caught and ended up in jail, our child would be declared a ward of the state. We instead named our children with first names we liked and chose their Hebrew names according to the departed relative tradition. Unfortunately, my son Alex does get teased a bit in religious school since his Hebrew name is Velvil. But, he still gets to tease the kid whose name is Pincus.

When our oldest son was about three we took a trip to the beach. We parked fairly far away and had to walk a good distance carrying our umbrella, chairs, sand toys, stroller, food, etc. Then we had to choose the perfect spot; close to the ocean, but not too close. As soon as we spread the blanket and set up the chairs, Eric informed us that he had to go pee pee. I didn't want to walk all the way back to the restroom so I let him know that he could pee in the ocean. He seemed surprised, but I informed him that whales pee in the ocean so it would be okay for him to do so. He held my hand and we walked towards the water. As soon as we arrived at the edge of the ocean, Eric began pulling down his bathing suit. "What are you doing?" I yelled. I had to teach him the protocol for peeing in the ocean. A guy (no matter what age) should walk into the ocean to at least waist level, then look around, whistle gleefully, say "What about those Mets?" and then take care of business.

I continued teaching Eric about life. A few years later after celebrating his sixth birthday, he asked me if he was old enough to see a PG-13 rated movie. I explained to him that he would need to be over 13 to be admitted. He thought for a while and then counted on his fingers and said with confidence, "So in seven years, I will be able to see any movie I want?" I wanted to "keep it real," so I let him know that he wouldn't be able to see an R-rated movie until he turned 17. He asked inquisitively, "What's in an R-rated movie?" I let him know that an R-rated movie contained very bad words and lots of fighting. He then proclaimed proudly, "So when I'm 17, I'll be able to see any movie I want."

I hated to burst his bubble, but I'm a stickler for the truth. "Eric," I said, "actually, you won't be able to see an X-rated movie until you are 18 years old. In fact it might be 21 in some states."

Quite surprised and somewhat frustrated, Eric asked, "Why Dad? What's so different about an X-rated movie?" I let him know that an X-rated movie contained very, very bad words and lot of fighting. In fact some of the fighting consisted of men and women fighting without wearing any clothes.

A few days later, I received a call at work from my wife. She was not her usual cheerful self. "Did you actually talk to our six year old about X-rated movies?" I stuttered a bit and mentioned that he initiated the conversation when he had asked me about the differences between the various movie ratings. It seemed that she just got a disturbing phone call from Eric's kindergarten teacher. The class was creating posters that showcased their most important wishes. Some kids wished that all the sick people they knew would get better. Still others wished for world peace. My son's poster showed two stick figures walking into a movie theater. Underneath, it said "I wish I could see an X-rated movie with my dad!!!"

I guess our young boy had grown up. It seemed like only months ago he was telling his friends how his favorite rock group was Foreigner and his favorite song was "Juice Box Hero."

Robin was not very happy with me. She was still a bit sore over the recent food drive incident. She collected bags of donated food on behalf of a local food bank. There were about 25 bags of groceries piled up on the floor of our living room. It was late at night and I was quite hungry. I took a gander at the donated food and noticed a package of Funyuns peeking out of one of the bags. I guess the noise of me crunching woke up Robin, and I was snagged.

This wasn't the only time my kids put me in embarrassing situations. After explaining the evils of smoking to our four year old son Alex, he went up to an old man smoking outside the mall. He said "You is smoking. You is gonna die!"

One time I accompanied my son Eric to a school event. The large Fortune 500 company I worked for at the time was just bought out by an even larger Fortune 50 company. I was introduced to the father of one of Eric's friends. He also worked in the same branch of the consumer package goods industry and was offering up some valuable information about the company I now worked for including how he knew many executives. He even offered to have me join some of these VIPs on the golf course. Eric promptly told the man that this wouldn't be necessary, as "Dad is hoping for a package."

When we took a family trip to Hilton Head Island, we were unexpectedly upgraded to a luxury suite. It had a view of the ocean, a pull-out Murphy bead and a bar complete with two stools! My son Alex opened the closet and said, "Wow! They even have a surf board for us." Alex emerged from the walk-in closet holding an ironing board. He had never seen one before.

When I was in fifth grade, one of the sixth graders had written the "F" bomb with chalk on the blacktop. My friends and I saw it. They seemed to be familiar with this word. I knew it was bad, but didn't quite understand why. When my father came home from work that evening, I had a private conversation with him and whispered the "F" word to him. He had me walk with him across the room to where some old books were on a shelf. He opened up his law dictionary and promptly read me the definition for the word "fornication." He let me know that what the kids wrote on the playground was slang. Fornication is the correct word and depending on the associated levels of consent and blood relations, it could be a crime in various states. I wasn't quite sure what he was talking about, but it did look like an important book.

I asked him if there were other bad words that he could explain to me. I thought this would help me become more popular at school. He let me know that bitch was actually just the name for a female dog. He warned me not to say Jesus Christ as this was saying the Lord's name in vain. Instead one could say cripes which was close, but did not convey the same degree of disrespect. I questioned Dad on this. "Dad, we're Jewish. I thought we don't believe that Jesus is our Lord."

He looked puzzled and said, "You may be right, but play it safe and use cripes instead." He then rattled off many other legal terms for various sexual acts.

The next day at school, an older tough kid was making fun of my dorky friends and me. He was cursing at us. I was the hero that day to my friends when I yelled back, "Sodomy!!" which was the legal term for "up yours."

# Scams & Pranks

L ike most people, I enjoy a good prank. It's always fun when one of Howard Stern's fans gets a *Baba Booey* in on the viewer call in portion of the Larry King show. Larry says "Hello Des Moines! You're on with Jesse Jackson." The caller sounds all serious, and then in the middle of the conversation throws in a *Baba Booey* and they quickly go to a commercial.

I participate in many conference calls at my job along with twenty or so colleagues from around the world all using the same dial in number. Sometimes the calls can get somewhat dry and need some excitement. I've always fantasized about breaking the ice by yelling *Baba Booey* in the middle of one of these calls. I'd disguise my voice and talk seriously about quarterly sales numbers in the Southern Cone region of South America and then when everyone is psyched about the boost in sales, I'd throw in my own hearty *Baba Booey*. So far, I've been able to curb my desire, since many people (especially those outside of the US) wouldn't understand the humor in it, and I'd be embarrassed to tell my family that I lost my job due to a prank phone call.

I did once accidently interrupt one of these conference calls. I was using my new wireless headphone and was not sure how to operate the mute button. I hit the button thinking I was muting my voice. I then coughed and hit the button again. A few people asked what that loud noise was. I ignored them.

By the way, why do people on conference calls consistently say "Sorry, can you please repeat the question? I was on mute." That's just a lame excuse; they didn't hear the question because they weren't listening!

I've decided to be a bit more serious on conference calls since the topic came up on my last performance appraisal:

*Larry's overuse of humor is annoying and detracts from the seriousness of his colleagues. For example, during a reorganization brainstorming session with the global business group, he suggested that Italy, France and Russia should be blended into the Salad Dressing region. Then when nobody laughed, he yelled, "What are you all on mute?" Actually, it is Larry who needs to be on mute more often.*

Back in college, my roommates and I lived in a basement apartment on campus. I had a sound effects record and my two roommates and I played it at maximum volume as students walked back from class. We left the apartment and hid behind trees to watch people's reactions to hearing the sounds of elephants, lions, a man coughing, a bowling strike followed by applause, a rooster crowing, a cuckoo clock striking twelve, a bugle call and rapid machine gun fire all echoing from our apartment window. Some people would just walk by and ignore it, while others would look around in case an elephant was actually on campus.

Suddenly, one of our roommates, Andy Robertson returned from class to our apartment. For whatever reason, he did not seem to notice the noise (at this point the record was playing the sounds of cows mooing) and sat down next to the stereo, reading the current issue of "Pit and Quarry" magazine (a standard for Mechanical Engineering majors). Now when people walked by, they would be shocked to hear glass breaking and upon looking in the window, see a guy quietly drinking a beer and reading a magazine. Then, all of a sudden, the sounds of twenty dogs barking would emerge from the apartment. We returned to the apartment and Andy calmly glanced at us, nodded and said "Hey hey hey" just like Dwayne in *"What's Happening?"*

For a while my son wanted to be an actor, and auditioned for many a school play. We explained to him that it was tough to be an actor and didn't want him to be disappointed if it didn't work out. He said,

"I know. If acting doesn't work out, I want to be an astronaut."

Once, while attending one of his performances, I tapped Robin on the shoulder and said, "Wouldn't it be cool if we started a wave like they do at baseball games?" She told me to either pay attention or go back to sleep, putting the kibosh on my wave plans.

A few months back, I was heavily into playing Texas Hold'em online. I wouldn't play for real money, but would have fun playing nonetheless. The other people at the table were playing on their computers from all over the world. There was a feature where you could chat with the other players. People would comment on what a lucky hand someone was dealt or deliver neighborly compliments like, "nice hand." My friends and I always played poker in college, but we now lived in different towns and it was quite a logistical mess to organize an in-person poker game. I thought it would be fun to get them all to the same online table.

One night we arranged to log on to a particular online poker website and all join a specific table. We did it at 10:00 PM after our kids and wives were asleep. Mitch, Dave, Danny and I all entered table #107 and we began to play poker. Unfortunately there were three other players at the table and we wanted it all to ourselves. We decided to utilize the chat feature to scare off the other players. I started the chat by saying "Anyone else gassy at this table, or is it just me?" Mitch quickly followed by chatting that he could smell it from his computer's speakers.

The strangers at our table did not appreciate this idle digestive chatter and chatted back, "Stop talking and start playing." We didn't.

In the middle of an exciting hand with a large pot and a possible straight flush battle with three players, Mitch chatted, "Does anyone else at this table regularly see corn in their doodie?" The others quickly left, and we had the table to ourselves; however it didn't seem quite as fun only concentrating on playing poker.

All the bathroom humor made me laugh quite loudly, and in doing so, I woke my wife. She didn't understand why I was laughing in my cramped office all alone. When I tried to explain, she couldn't fathom how guys in their mid 40's could find so much pleasure in annoying and/or boring other internet poker players who were probably only 14 years old. Maybe she didn't understand it, but we all had a ton of fun.

I began to think how my friends and I would continue to have fun in our golden years. It then hit me like a ton of bricks. Just like we need to plan for our retirement financially, we need to plan for it socially as well. Yes, I would spend quality time with my wife and enjoy vacations that would include visits with our children and hopefully some cute grandchildren. But what would we do for serious fun? We would need a retirement plan for our social future. Although our wives love us (or at least pretend to), none of us thought they'd want us home every day watching TV and planning what early bird special we would eat at 3:00 PM. We would need part-time jobs to keep peace within our marriages and ensure we got enough fraternal fun.

Our working years were the perfect time to invest in our social 401K. How could my fellow immature friends and I have fun when we retire? We decided we would buy stock in companies that are headquartered in the New York City metro area. We would accumulate single shares of stock from corporations within the tri-state area with thoughts of our retirement. This would allow us to attend the annual shareholder meetings of every company within our portfolio.

We would dress up in suits, meet at the train station sporting briefcases, and catch the 8:15 into the city (like the BTO song). We'd pay senior citizen fares which would be kind to our fixed income budgets. Once at the meetings, we'd load up on coffee, muffins, and all the other freebies that the shareholders receive. We'd even be old enough to capitalize on the benefits of the sole prune Danish pastry that was always left behind. We'd have fun betting amongst ourselves as to which one of us could cough the loudest, ask the stupidest question to members of the board, collect the most business cards or fit the most extra food in our valises. Not only would it give us something to do and get us out of our houses, but we'd enjoy each other's company and continue to have an outlet for our immaturity well into our mid 80's.

We'd also occasionally crash conferences and seminars, kind of like wedding crashers only more desperate. We'd pick up lots of pens, memo pads and enter drawings to win computer software that we would promptly sell on eBay. It's not like we would need data mining tools or sales management software at our age. We'd be more interested in suppositories than data repositories.

I guess I inherited my panache for pranks from my father. Eight days after our second son was born, we, like most Jews, had a Bris (ritual circumcision) in our home. The mohel is the person who is specially trained to perform this delicate procedure and conduct the religious ceremony. We used the same mohel who circumcised our first son, who just happened to be the brother of comedian Jackie Mason. He interrogated me on the type of gauze pads that we had purchased. He said that he clearly asked for 4-by-4 inch pads but we had 2-by-2s, and that he would have to make do with them, but next time we should follow his exact instructions. He sounded just like his brother except his material wasn't as funny.

Dad made a beeline to him and said, "Rabbi, I'm a big fan of your brother Jackie." Then without warning, Dad pulled a small device from his pocket and showed it to the mohel. It was about the size of garage door opener, had a small speaker and a button and had "Jackie Mason's Final Word" written on it. Pressing the button played a recording of none other than Jackie Mason. My father then began to press the button, and the device emitted such gems as, "Are you always this stupid?" or "You're a schmuck, the biggest!" He pressed it again and we heard, "Screw you and your friend too!" and "Oy is this a putz."

The rabbi became visibly annoyed and said, "I find this to be quite vulgar."

Dad didn't stop, he continued to press the buttons in a rapid fashion and kept repeating, "What about this one?" I had to intercept and begged my father to at least wait until after the mohel cut his grandson's foreskin before playing any more quotes from his toy. Luckily things worked out okay. As soon as the circumcision was complete, my son Alex showed his dismay by peeing profusely. I suddenly understood why the larger gauze pads were necessary.

I should have taken my dad's behavior as a warning to be careful with my pranks. I had just upgraded my computer with a sound card (brand new technology in 1990). Now I could play computer games with real sound. The sound card came with some bonus applications and my favorite was the "text-to-speech" tool. If you typed "Hello ladies and gentleman" and pressed Enter, a computerized voice would speak them out of the computer speaker. The voice reminded me of the robot on "Lost in Space." It wasn't too long before I was typing and the computer was speaking foul and disgusting sentences. I decided to type some really bad stuff and add some extra characters for emphasis. I typed, "F*** Youuuuuuuuuuu" and added a few more expletives for good luck. I then called my friend Mike, whom I knew would appreciate this. He wasn't home and when his answering machine beeped, I hit Enter and the computer voice spewed my message over the phone.

I waited all night, but Mike didn't call me back. Did he really think someone other than me left this message? What could he have been doing that was more important than calling be back to say how funny this message was? Two days went by and I finally called him. He answered the phone rather quietly which was unusual for Mike. I said, "Michael?"

He replied, "Hi Larry." I quickly asked if he received the message I left on his answering machine. He then said in a quiet voice, "Arlene is in the hospital. She had a ruptured ovarian cyst that had to be removed." I made sure his wife was okay and conveyed my best wishes for a speedy recovery. I then quickly asked what he thought of my message. He said it was okay, but didn't rave about it like I thought he would.

# Cup or Cone

It was a hot summer day and a few of us decided to take a break from work in the office and visit a local ice cream shop. As soon as we opened the door, we were greeted by a strong pungent odor. It wasn't that of chocolate or vanilla, but it reeked like something was dead. Most sane people would have just turned around and left this establishment and visited another of the many ice cream parlors near our office. But we were with Matt Heimlich.

Matt was always eager to help his fellow man. He looked at the nondescript man behind the counter and knew he needed to inform him of the stench. The proprietor was Indian, Pakistani or possibly Mexican, but his weak command of the English language didn't provide any clues of his nationality. In any event, Matt approached the counter and said matter-of-factly, "Sir, are you aware that something smells really bad in here?"

The man nodded as if he understood the severity of the situation, and responded with a single question. "Ka-up oor Ko-in?" he said and smiled.

*This page intentionally left blank*

Matt was up to the challenge. He explained in great detail to the confused man that an animal might have died within the walls; possibly a rat, and there might very well be a ton of maggots and flies within the walls. Obviously, this was not good for business and the situation needed to be rectified immediately. Once again, the man nodded eagerly, held his ice cream scooper at full attention and said, "Ka-up oor Ko-in?"

Unwilling to give up this great opportunity to help the ice cream shop remain in business, Matt sternly suggested that the situation be addressed before the board of health showed up and closed down the establishment. The man became somewhat impatient as he looked at Matt and said strongly with much conviction, "Ka-up oor Ko-in?"

Matt finally gave up and begrudgingly said, "I'll have a cup of chocolate marshmallow."

The man smiled and said, "Sprinkles; chocolate or rainbow"? Matt chose rainbow sprinkles. The storekeeper served him his cup of ice cream and then looked at our colleague Mo Samuels, and said, "Ka-up oor Ko-in?"

The ice cream shop shortly closed due to lack of business most likely attributed to the bad smell. It took a while for the storekeeper to find an alternative career but he finally did. He is now gainfully employed in an upscale designer lingerie boutique. When a customer shows some interest in the store's Madonna inspired bra collection, our friend smiles and says, "Ka-up oor Ko-in?" "Cup or Cone?"

# Put It In Your Act!

I've often mentioned to my family that I'd like to perform a stand-up comedy routine sometime in my life. I even signed up for a comedy class given at a local community college years ago, but I only lasted two classes before dropping out. At the initial class, the instructor let us know that all comedy is derived from tragedy, sadness and pain. That didn't sound very funny. One of my classmates quickly agreed with the teacher and told the class of his multiple failed attempts at suicide. That definitely wasn't very funny.

At the next class, the teacher told us of the dark underbelly of the comedy business. He let us know that it would take months to even get a 15 minute act together. After practicing the act, it would no longer be funny to you, but you'd still have to pretend that it was when performing it to an audience over and over. He then talked about a forming a business plan, and tactics of how to sell yourself to the comedy club booking agents. There was nothing funny about this class and I never returned.

Since then, whenever I come up with something I think is funny, my kids yell "N F!" which stands for "not funny." My wife is slightly more supportive and yells, "Put it in your act!"  Hence: the title of this book.

Here's a collection of items that aren't big enough to have their own chapters in this book, but someday will be the crux of my stand-up comedy act.

Every time I saw comedians perform at various comedy clubs they were always hilarious. That was until one spring night when I attended a comedy performance.  You see, my allergies were pretty bad and I had to take some strong medication.  This prevented me from drinking any alcohol. It was that night that I realized that most people laugh because they have downed a few rounds of drinks and are somewhat looped.  To make the rest of this chapter more enjoyable, I recommend that you stop reading now, have about three stiff martinis and then continue.  Now I don't condone underage drinking, so if you're under 21, please fix your parents the martinis and have them read you the rest of the book.

Now that you have been properly medicated, here is the act:

Reinforcements – I've often heard presidents and generals stating that we're sending in

*This page intentionally left blank*

reinforcements to the troops, to our allies and to the victims of natural disasters. Why are we doing this? Shouldn't we send them ammunition, food or medicine? Even if they all have loose leaf notebooks, don't they have bigger problems than fixing torn pages with reinforcements?

Then I'd talk about the interviews with the winner of a boxing match or a team's MVP. Everybody is thanking Jesus or Allah for allowing them to emerge victorious and win the big game. For once, I'd like to see a Jewish guy being interviewed after winning an international chess tournament. He'd shout into the microphone, "I just want to thank the man upstairs, Moses, his brother Aaron and the patriarchs, Abraham, Isaac and my main man Jacob for allowing me to move my knight to king's bishop 4 for the checkmate."

Once the laughter subsided, I would break out some of my impersonations. Most comedians do a few good impressions of famous people. In order to be unique, I would impersonate dot matrix printers of the late '80s and early '90s. Ladies and gentleman, here's my rendition of an Epson FX-80. Rrrrrrrrrrrrrr, Ehhhhhhhhhhhh, Rrrrrrrrrrrrrrrr, Ehhhhhhhhhhhh (once again, I would have to wait for the abundant laughter to subside). Now, here's an Okidata Daisy Wheel impact printer! Ieeeeeeeeee Owwwwwwwwwwww Ieeeeeee Owwwwwwwww.

I would then ask for a moment of silence for a LaserJet III (Get it? No sound).

I've been fine-tuning my act for so long, that my material is somewhat dated. It's stuck in 1983 just like my music and clothing. As I strived for perfection in my comedy act for the past 20+ years, the people I would impersonate have unfortunately passed on. Hopefully my audience would still remember them or maybe they'd understand the jokes the next day after talking to their aging grandparents.

My next bit involves two celebrities in a fictitious situation. Let's imagine, if you will, that Menachem Begin, the sixth Prime Minister of Israel visited Julia Child's "French Chef" cooking show. She would be facing the camera in front of her well stocked kitchen. She'd introduce Menachem and he would shuffle in and mutter something under his breath that sounded like a cross between a hello and a cough.

She would then ask Menachem if he likes bacon. He would explain he never had it since it's not kosher, but has been told it tasted like fried pastrami and resembles something he once sampled at a UJA benefit breakfast in Brooklyn called Sizzlean. After a bit of coaxing from Julia he would agree to try it and the studio audience would break out in applause (all three of them).

Julia wouldn't simply fry the bacon as that would be too pedestrian. She would use an old family French technique to roast the bacon at a low temperature in an oven, slowly until it develops a rich complex and smoky taste and crispy texture. She would then beckon, "Oh Menachem" in her thick French accent. "Oh Menachem, Men-ach- chem!!!.

He'd mutter, "vut?"

She would then look directly into the camera and at Menachem slightly crossing her eyes and say, "Are you **begging** to **begin baking bacon Begin**?"

Just when my crowd was recovering from their laughter, I would hit them with this doozie:

Ladies and gentleman, when I arrived at this beautiful comedy club, I was a bit early. I had about 65 minutes to kill with nothing to do. What did I see right across the street but a "one hour Martinizing" place. Wow – One hour is perfect. That would still give me five minutes to cross the street, do a sound check and get acclimated to the stage. I didn't know what

Martinizing actually was, but I was eager to find out. I entered the cleaning establishment and told the person behind the counter that I wanted to have my shirt Martinized. She looked at me slightly puzzled as I took my shirt off and gave it to her. I told her I'd be waiting and sat down shirtless and read a newspaper. As advertised, as soon as sixty minutes elapsed, she hit the bell and said, "Sir, your shirt is ready."

I approached the counter, paid her $3.75 and she gave me my shirt on a hanger covered with plastic. I unwrapped it, threw away the hanger and plastic and then it hit me. My beautiful white shirt had freakin' *Martin* written all over it!!!!!!

I would wave to the audience saying "That's all I have tonight. Don't forget to tip your waitresses."

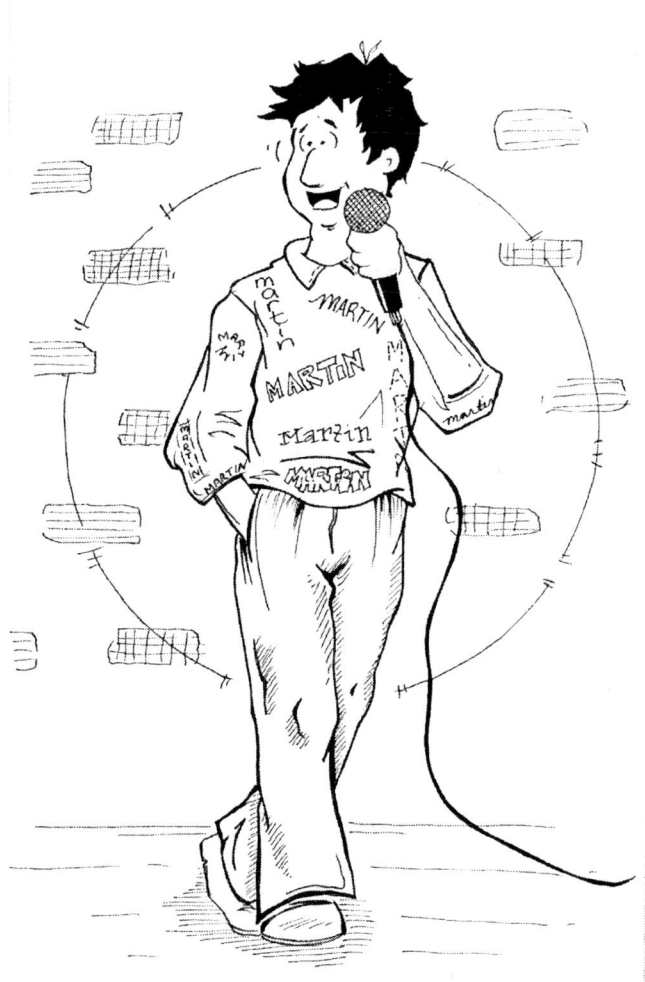

# Epilogue

Well, I've completed one of my important life goals in writing this book. Yes, I'm blessed with a terrific family, a rewarding career and great friends. And now, to top it all off, a book. I have also completed yet another life goal – to exceed 50 pages. In literary speak, this milestone allows "Put It In Your Act!" to be a fully bound book. Anything less than 50 pages would be subject to an embarrassingly amateurish spiral bound, which in my view is nothing less than a glorified pamphlet. To keep my effort professional, I decided not to mess with cheesy fonts like *comic sans*. I did briefly toy with the idea of using `courier` since I'm a big tennis fan, but I liked John McEnroe more than Jim Courier and he has yet to have his own font.

I had a distant relative who by the way had the exact same name as my father, Arthur Osman. He achieved a small degree of notoriety as an influential participant in New York labor as he founded and led the Department Store Workers' Union. My dad had always said that we had a famous relative who had written a book. One day I found this "so called" book in my parents' garage next to some Frisbees and wiffle balls, and it did tell the story of UAW Local 65's creation in 1933. However it was not a book. It was at best a brochure with three staples keeping the ten pages together.

I could have easily slapped together 24 pages and then included an additional 26 pages of filler that all read, "this page intentionally left blank," however I decided to take the high road (just a few pages of filler). When my descendants find copies of this book in their respective basements next to their forgotten and long abandoned possessions, at least it will be a real book.

# Dedication

I'd like to thank my friends and family for supporting my efforts in writing this book or at least pretending to support me. For years, my wife would exclaim after one of my bizarre observations, "Put it in Your Act!" or "Add it to your book!" I have fond recollections of my Grandma Gussie saying, "What a day I had with Max; I could write a book."

Max heard her and said, "So Gussie, why don't you write this book?"

I remember my English professor at Rutgers College in the required expository (we called it suppository) writing class commenting on my paper, "Very funny, C-." I always felt I'd get a B- if I left my jokes out of the paper. All these little events inspired me to just go for it.

The real thanks go to my wife Robin. While I spent my time writing this book, collecting Mr. Peanut stuff, trying to recreate whatever recipes I watched on Food TV, playing guitar and piano, playing online poker, watching old Match Game episodes on the Game Show Network, or just sitting around doing nothing, she was busy raising our three beautiful children. She drove the car pools (both ways and uphill), baked the brownies, attended the plays, marching band competitions, gymnastic exhibitions, and tallis making classes and washed my underwear all in her spare time. She will also risk jeopardizing her career, when she asks all her co-workers to purchase copies of this book and then have to face them after they read it. This will be her own personal walk of shame.

# Book Club Discussion Questions

What specific themes did the author emphasize throughout the novel? What do you think he is trying to convey to the reader?

Do the characters seem real and believable? Can you relate to their predicaments? To what extent do they remind you of yourself or someone you know?

Did certain parts of the book make you uncomfortable? If so, why did you feel that way?

Did this lead to a new understanding or awareness of some aspect of your life that you might not have thought about before, or did it just plain skeeve you out?

Do you find yourself more interested in how food changes the attributes of your urine?

If so, you might want serve the members of your book club a special meal. Serve up large quantities of asparagus and beets, and wash it all down with some strong fresh brewed espresso. Don't drink any water, as this will dilute the end result. After your discussion, have the group visit the restroom either individually or as a group.

What did you notice? Discuss.